KARATE KIDS 101 BEGINNERS GUIDE TO TRADITIONAL STYLE KARATE
Yasushi Abe
Yukari Abe
Taito Abe

Find us on the web at: http://karatekid.info/

Photographs and book layout by Michael J. Kulyk.
Translation from Japanese to English by Sherry L. Kulyk.

Contents

Hello Everyone,

Thank you for taking an interest in this book. I decided to publish this book because I want to share the greatness of karate with as many people as possible. Karate is a magical tool that will make your life a happy one.

First of all, let me share some traits that I have gained from karate: Self confidence, courage, physical agility, health, youth, many friendships, happiness, and much more. I learned and gained many things from karate. Now it's your turn.

This book teaches the basics of karate. If you find joy in it, please continue to learn karate.

Nothing is required to do karate. No special equipment is required to practice and you can practice by yourself or with friends.

Karate uses the entire body. Right hand, left hand, right foot, left foot. You will enhance your balancing skills. The coordination you gain from practicing karate will help you excel in any sport.

In addition to training the body, karate can be played as a game with friends. Kata (karate moves) are like gymnastics or ice skating in which you compete for performance points. Kumite (sparring) is like fencing or judo in which you compete by accumulating attack points.

One way of practicing karate is through memorizing kata or "karate moves." Kata plays an important role in traditional karate because it is image training. You imagine blocking, punching, kicking your opponent.

Kata will become fun as you practice more. Why? Because the story behind your imagination while performing kata is that you will always win. It is fun to imagine beating your opponent. You are always the hero.

This book introduces the basics of karate--punches, blocks, kicks, and stances--that kata are built upon, as well as how to tie a belt, how to bow, and how to sit.

This unique style of martial arts was founded with the collaboration of Chinese and Okinawa martial arts, but is now practiced and enjoyed by many around the world.

To enjoy karate as a sport is a good thing. I love it, and I enjoy watching karate exhibitions and performing karate demonstrations. However, I feel the benefits of karate do not stop here.

The real purpose behind karate is not fighting; rather it is about being able to defend yourself and your family if necessary.

Our Mission

We, members of Shingetsuryu, uphold traditional style karate by concentrating on the basis of karate: kata. The Shingetsuryu style is strengthening components physically and artistically while being able to defend oneself. Introducing this to the world is our mission.

Karate is for everyone. Children as young as 4 years old can start if parent(s) participate. In my classes there are lots of 4-year old karate kids. How about senior citizens? Of course they can practice too. They become healthier, younger, and full of energy.

Are you full of stress? Practicing even a little karate a few days a week will allow you to sleep better.

This book is for all, including those who are thinking about starting karate and to those beginners already practicing karate. Karate teachers can use this book as a textbook also.

In our effort to create an easy-to-use karate book, we have included many pictures and detailed explanations.

Finally, I mentioned that karate is a magical tool that will make your life a happy one. Karate is an great way to promote emotional and physical health by allowing you to relieve the stresses and frustrations of daily life. By continuously practicing karate, you will learn to think with a clear mind and feel healthier.

There is no expensive equipment involved, and you can practice even in a small area, You can practice by yourself or with friends. You can enhance your balancing skills. You can practice as a means of dieting, You will be able to defend yourself if you have to. You can practice at your own pace. Aren't these all great points?

When you share common interests, you will gain friends even throughout the world. Friends who sweat together will be friends forever. In Mar 2011, there was a big earthquake in Japan, and I received many words of encouragement from friends around the world. You too will make many friends throughout the world just by sharing a common interest in karate.

Change in Logo

In Dec 2010, the kanji characters in the logo mark changed. In my continuous quest to perfect karate, I changed the character" 新" (pronounced shin) which means "new" to"真" (also pronounced shin) which means "truth".

Yasushi Abe

Introductions

Yasushi Abe

Yasushi Abe was born in 1959 in Tokyo, Japan.

Having a father who was a Chinese martial artist as well as a judo wrestler, Yasushi Abe naturally grew interest in the world of martial arts.

Prior to engaging in karate, he was interested in judo and boxing. Training began in his high school days. During high school, he figured boxing will be useful in fights and learned to fight on his own. During college, he entered Kaneko Gym, a professional gym taught by an east asian champion.

He was on the judo team, but,was scouted by the weightlifting team because of his superior lower body strength. He participated in two high school com-

Introductions

petitions. He has won the championship in competitions including regular adult competitors as well. He competed in the lightest weight class, the fly-weight (under 52 kg), and was the tallest competitor in high school.

There was an episode in which there were two brawls during his high school days. Seven opponents versus himself. In both cases, he defeated the opponents' leader within one minute.

After graduating from Nihon University with a degree in Physical Education in 1982, he worked as a physical education teacher in Tokyo. In 1983, he started learning Shito Ryu style karate. He won a kumite tournament in Musashimurayama City and joined their kumite team.

He won 8 consecutive times at the All Japan Teacher competition, surpassing the "King of Kata," Sakumoto sensei's record.
He was awarded the Renshi

license by the Japan Karatedo Federation. This certification is only given to select certified All Japan referees that have achieved over 5th level (godan). In addition, the Renshi license is only awarded to a chosen few individuals.

Abe sensei has been active as the vice referee for the all Japan High School Karatedo for Tokyo City. Through interactions with all the high school karate instructors across Japan, he researched traditional kata and martial art styles. His profound knowledge of karate can be said to have stemmed from here.

He taught karate to five of his children who all became Tokyo City champions. His family was able to enjoy the only male championship trophy and the only female championship trophy at the same time.

Introductions

# Yukari Abe

Yukari Abe started karate at 4 years old.

She became a 9-time champion from 1st grade to 9th grade in Tokyo, the most populated city in Japan. Her record has not been broken up to this date.

She was recruited by a highly-coveted girls karate school in high school and entered inter-high school competition. Unfortunately, having endured vigorous practice, her knee gave out, ending her career as a martial artist. She has fully recovered since then and currently enjoys a fun karate.

Taito Abe

Taito Abe, Yukari's younger brother, started karate at 3 years old.

When he was 4, he did an up and over gymnastic pole move, or "saka agari" 12 consecutive times without touching the ground with his foot. (Saka agari is a common test of agility for Japanese children.)

He was a Tokyo kata and kumite champion. His specialty in kumite was kicking and he even won a match using a round-house kick that he learned the day before the competition.

He is currently training to become an all around martial artist professional.

Shingetsu ryu Roots

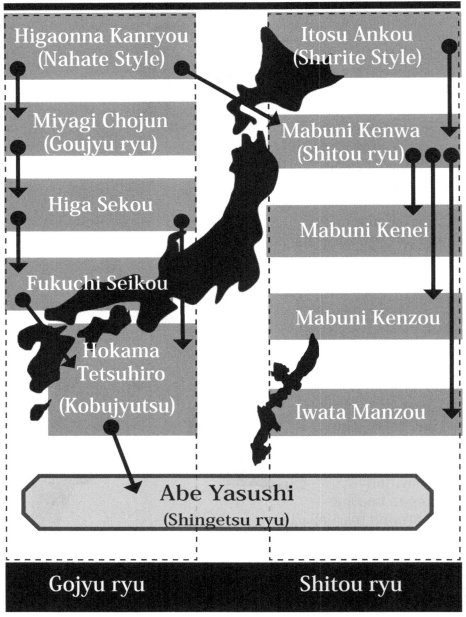

Higaonna Kanryou
(Nahate Style)

Itosu Ankou
(Shurite Style)

Miyagi Chojun
(Goujyu ryu)

Mabuni Kenwa
(Shitou ryu)

Higa Sekou

Mabuni Kenei

Fukuchi Seikou

Mabuni Kenzou

Hokama
Tetsuhiro
(Kobujyutsu)

Iwata Manzou

Abe Yasushi
(Shingetsu ryu)

Gojyu ryu

Shitou ryu

# Shingetsu ryu Policy

- Preserve traditional karate to pass on to younger generations

- Promote a healthy heart and body via karate practices

- Use karate only to uphold justice

- Practice safe and peaceful karate to avoid unnecessary fights

- Practice rationally

- Always respect your practice opponent and be well-mannered

- Be a contribution to society

Lesson 1: How To Tie a Belt (beginner)

Obi

Karate uniforms or "karate-gi" require a belt or "obi".

There are two ways to tie a belt--beginners and advanced styles. In the beginner's style, the belt remains crossed on the back (step 27); whereas in the advanced style it is flush (see pg. 21).

Fold belt in half

Hold belt in place

Place belt below navel

Wrap both ends of belt around back and cross it

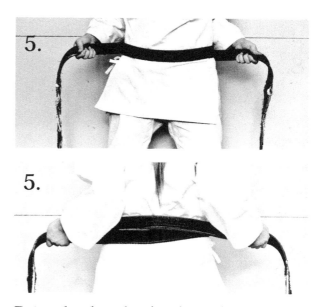

Bring both sides back to the front

Lesson 1: How To Tie a Belt (beginner)

6.

Place the belt pulled from the right to the center of your body.

7.

8.

Holding right hand still, place the belt from the left on top.

9.

Place the belt from the left on top and cross it over.

Slide the right hand belt up between the belt and gi.

10.

Holding the belt with left hand, pull right belt up all the way through upwards.

11.

12.

Pull right hand up towards right shoulder and left hand belt towards left thigh.

Lesson 1: How To Tie a Belt (beginner)

13.

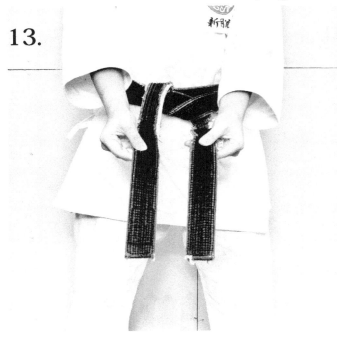

Adjust the belts to equal length.

14.

Hold the belt with left hand as shown and flip it up.

15.

Bring flipped belt forward.

Holding left
hand still,
bring up
closer to
right belt.

Bring the
right belt
down over
left hand belt
to create a
loop.

Holding the
right hand
still, put left
hand in the
loop.

Lesson 1: How To Tie a Belt (beginner)

19.

With the hand in loop, grab the top of the belt.

20.

Pull through the belt grabbed by the left hand.

21.

Keep pulling belt up through loop.

Pull belt
all the way
through and
upwards.

22.

23.

Pull left hand
up towards
left shoulder,
and right
hand down
towards right
thigh.

Confirm that
belts are
equal length.

24.

15

Lesson 1: How To Tie a Belt (beginner)

25.

Tighten belt by pulling tightly outwards.

26.

Again, check to see if belts are equal length. If not, redo previous steps.

27.

The belt
should look
like this from
the front.
make sure
the belt knot
is slightly
below navel.

27.

The belt
should be
crossed at
the center of
back.

Lesson 1: How To Tie a Belt (advanced)

Obi

This is the advanced way to tie obi. As seen here, the back of the belt is a doubled up clean and flush.

Hold the left end of the belt leaving a tail the lengh of the desired length of the finished belt.

Holding the belt with the left hand, wrap the right end of the belt behind back.

Switch hands and grab the right end of belt with left hand.

Cross left hand over the right end of the belt and switch hands, holding belt below navel.

Wrap long end of belt around back overlapping over the belt below.

Bring belt back around towards front and hand off to left hand.

Lesson 1: How To Tie a Belt (advanced)

7.

Place the belt pulled from the right to the center of your body.

8.

Holding right hand still, place the belt from the left on top.

9.

10.

Place the belt from the left on top and cross it over.

Slide the right hand belt up between the belt and gi.

Holding the belt with left hand, pull right belt up all the way through upwards.

Pull right hand up towards right shoulder and left hand belt towards left thigh.

21

Lesson 1: How To Tie a Belt (advanced)

14.

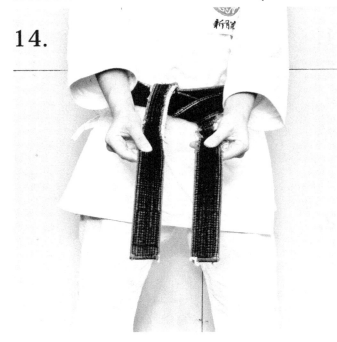

Adjust the belts to equal length.

15.

Hold the belt with left hand as shown and flip it up.

16.

Bring flipped belt forward.

Holding left
hand still,
bring up
closer to
right belt.

Bring the
right belt
down over
left hand belt
to create a
loop.

Holding the
right hand
still, put left
hand in the
loop.

Lesson 1: How To Tie a Belt (advanced)

20.

With the hand in loop, grab the top of the belt.

21.

Pull through the belt grabbed by the left hand.

22.

Keep pull-ing belt up through loop.

Pull belt all the way through and upwards.

23.

24.

Pull left hand up towards left shoulder, and right hand down towards right thigh.

Confirm that belts are equal length.

25.

Lesson 1: How To Tie a Belt (advanced)

26.

Tighten belt by pulling tightly outwards.

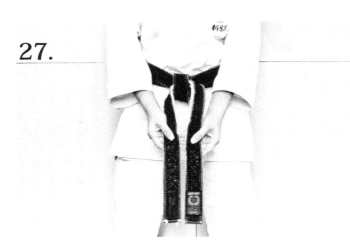

27.

Again, check to see if belts are equal length. If not, redo previous steps.

28.

The belt
should look
like this from
the front.
make sure
the belt knot
is slightly
below navel.

28.

Rear view
should look
like this.

Ritsurei

Bowing then standing at attention is called ritsurei. Martial arts begin and end with a bow (rei).

Bowing not only shows your opponent that you are serious, but also serves as a sign of respect.

Bow before entering and leaving the dojo.

Bow as a sign of appreciation and gratitude. Do not bow with hands together.

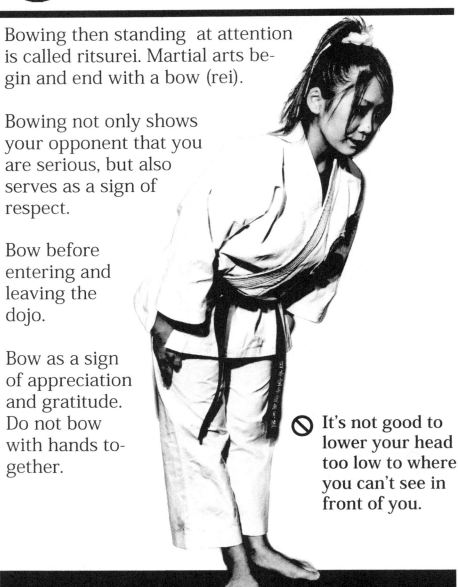

🚫 It's not good to lower your head too low to where you can't see in front of you.

Without bending your back, bow (head to hips should be straight) at a 45 degree angle and lower your head.

31

Lesson 2: Reihou 1(Ritsurei)

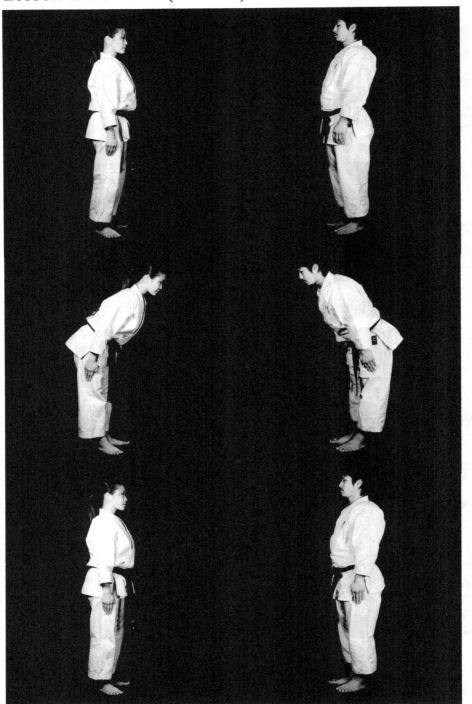

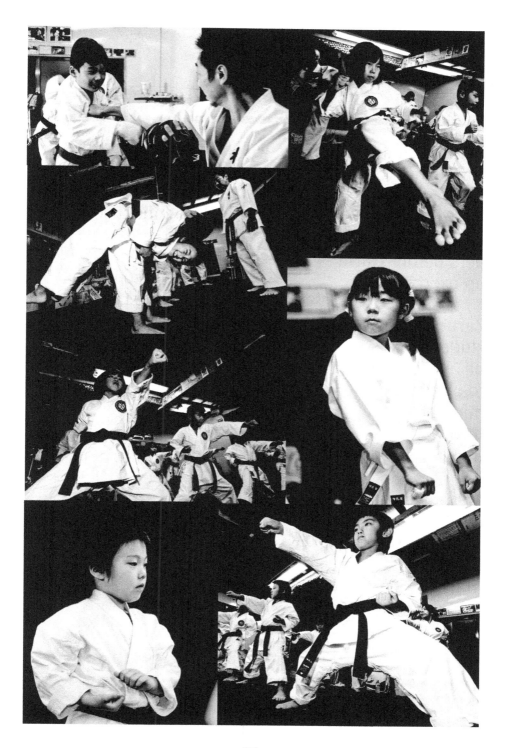

Zarei

Karate training starts with zarei--to sit at attention and bow--to the instructor (sensei) as well as to training partners before warm up exercises.

Zarei also includes mokusou or "meditation" to clear the mind before training.

Start out by standing at attention (musubi dachi). Next, put left knee on floor then the right knee and stand on both knees. Finally, slowly sit, mokusou, then bow.

Students also bow before entering the training area (dojo), as well as before leaving the dojo.

36

Stand at attention
(musubidachi)

Bring left knee
down.

Put left knee on
floor.

Lesson 2: Reihou (Zarei)

4.

5.

6.

Put right knee on floor and stand on both knees.

Standing on knees, straighten ankles.

Sit and place hands on top of upper thighs. This position is called seiza. Meditation (mokusou) also happens here.

Place left hand on floor.

Place right hand on floor, touching index fingers and thumbs to form a triangle.

Bend arms and lower head. Do not raise buttocks,

Lesson 2: Reihou (Zarei)

Straighten both arms and say either "onegaishimasu" (please) or "ariga-tougozaimashita" (thank you).

Retract right arm..

Retract left arm and place both hands on upper thighs.

13.

14.

15.

Straighten your
ankles and sit up,
standing on both
knees.

Standing on both
knees, bend both
ankles

Raise right knee
first.

Lesson 2: Reihou (Zarei)

16.

17.

Raise left knee and
stand up.

Stand at atten-
tion.
(musubidachi)

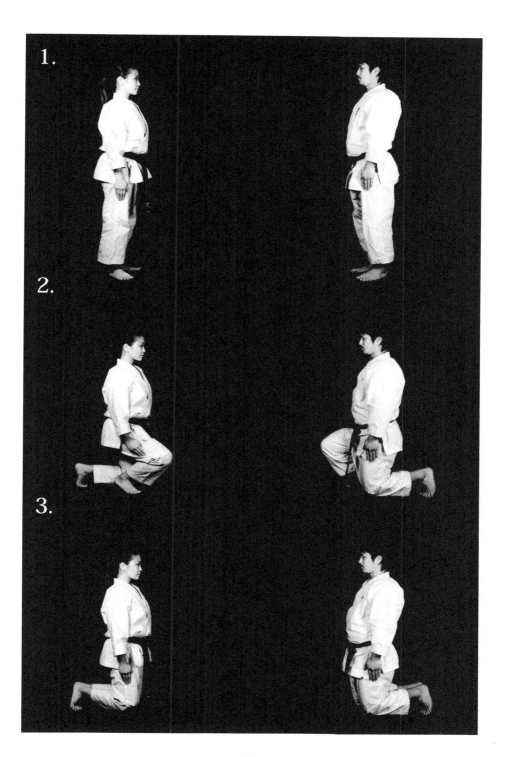

1.

2.

3.

Lesson 2: Reihou (Zarei)

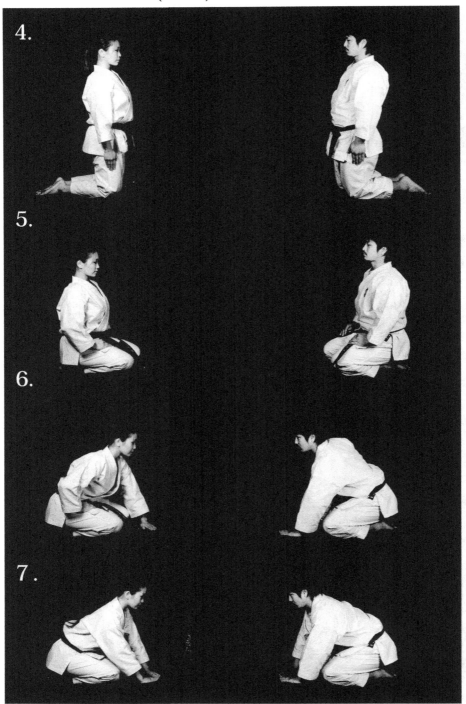

4.

5.

6.

7.

8.

9.

10.

11.

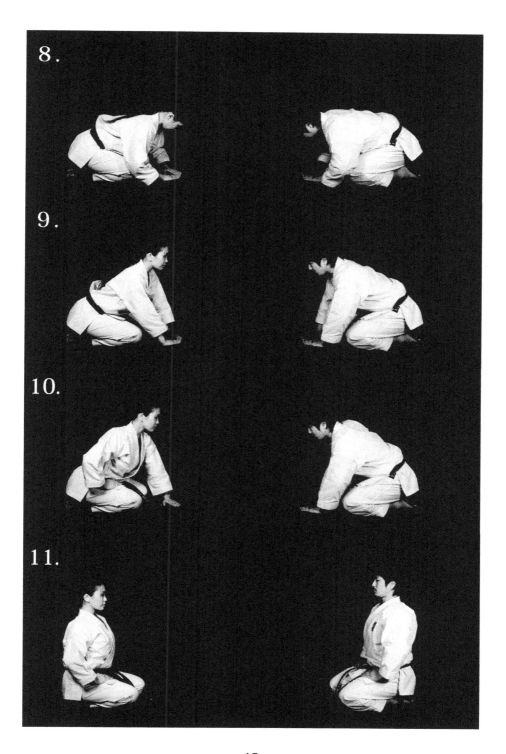

Lesson 2: Reihou (Zarei)

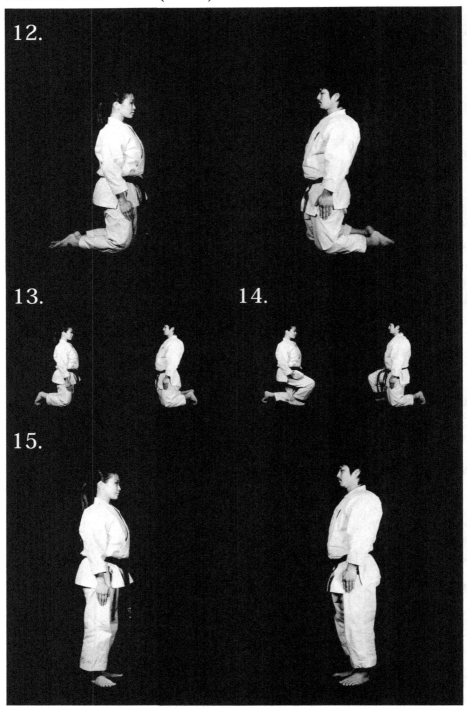

12.

13.

14.

15.

Tachi Kata

There are many ways to stand or "tachi kata" in karate. This lesson covers 18 tachi katas:

1. Heisoku Dachi
2. Musubi Dachi
3. Heikou Dachi
4. Hachiji Dachi
5. Naihanchi Dachi
6. Shiko Dachi
7. Kiba Dachi
8. Moto Dachi
9. Zenkutsu Dachi
10. Koukutsu Dachi
11. Hamni Koukutsu Dachi
12. Renoji Dachi
13. Nekoashi Dachi
14. Kousa Dachi
15. Bensoku Dachi
16. Sagiashi Dachi
17. Kake Sagiashi Dachi
18. Sanchin Dachi

1. Heisoku Dachi

Stand with
feet together.

Lesson 3: Stances (tachi kata)

2. Musubi Dachi

Stand with heels together and toes open at a 30 or 45 degree angle. This is basically standing at attention.

3. Heikou Dachi

Standing
with the
outer edge of
the feet be-
ing parallel.

4. Hachiji Dachi

Standing similar to musubi dachi but with feet at shoulder width apart.

Stance can also be called Soto-Hachiji-Dachi.
.

5. Naihanchi Dachi

The outer edge of feet should be anywhere from parallel to 10 degrees inwards. The feet should be a little wider than shoulder width. Do not bend knees inwards. Keep tension in legs by pulling outwards.

This stance is also called Uchi-Hachiji-Dachi.

6. Shiko Dachi

Similar to Hachiji-Dachi stance but with feet at one and a half to double the width apart. Don't bend knees inwards. Try as much as possible to face it outwards. Both feet should be facing outwards at a 30 to 45 degree angle.

7. Kiba Dachi

Naihanchi-Dachi stance but with feet at one and a half to double the width. Similar to Shiko Dachi but point toes inwards while the soles face outwards with both feet positioned parallel to 10 degree inwards. Do not bend knees inwards.

Lesson 3: Stances (tachi kata)

8. Moto Dachi

From the front, the legs are shoulder width apart, while both feet are spaced at shin length from the knees to the floor. Straighten the rear leg and slightly bend the front legs, putting a little weight on it. Without bending the lower half of your body, point your navel forward.

9. Zenkutsu Dachi

From the front, the legs should be shoulder width apart, with the feet at same spacing as moto dachi plus one step more forward. As moto-dachi, weight should be placed in the front leg as it is slightly bent. Without twisting lower half of your body, point navel forwards.

10. Koukutsu Dachi

Stance is the same as Zenkutsu Da- chi but with body twisted to face for- ward.

11. Hanmi Koukutsu Dachi

Place rear leg so that it is perpendicular to the front legs. Rear knee should be bent to the side while the front knee should be bent facing forward. Lower hips without raising heel of foot in front. Feet width should be a little narrower than shiko dachi. Avoid pointing your navel over 45 degrees to the side but try to point it as forward as possible.

12. Renoji Dachi

Place your rear foot at a 45 degree angle. Front leg should be relaxed and placed forward naturally. Raise heel of front foot slightly. The inner edge of both feet should be at a 45 degree angle to each other.

13. Nekoashi Dachi

From the renoji stance, lower hips, with knees bent forward at a 45 degree angle and front knee facing forward. The inner edges of both feet should be 45 degrees to each other. While avoiding attacks to the lower half of the body, this stance enables swift kicks. It doesn't allowe the upper body to fall back.

14. Kousa Dachi

Place front foot directly forward, lower hips, and place rear knee to where it will sit behind front knee. Rear foot should be placed at a 45 degree angle from the front foot with the heel of the foot raised. This stance enables swift moving to the rear.

15. Bensoku Dachi

From Kousa Dachi, place the rear foot a little closer to the front foot. Face the front foot slightly in-wards while the the rear foot is placed parallel to the front foot.

This stance is used when throwing an opponent or to spin around to change direc-tions.

16. Sagiashi Dachi

Stand on one foot and raise knee up high. Place inner side of foot of raised leg on the supporting leg. This stance not only avoids attacks to lower half of the body but also serves as the initial move to kick or step forward to attack.

17. Kake Sagiachi Dachi

Same as
Sagiashi
dachi only
the raised
foot is tucked
behind the
knee of the
supporting
leg.

18. Sanchin Dachi

Feet should be shoulder width apart, with front foot placed slightly above the other foot and faced inwards. The toes of rear foot should be facing forward.

Looking from the side, the toes of rear foot should be parallel to the heel of the front foot. Bend toes as if to grab the floor, tightening muscles on lower half of body. Slightly bend knees inwards with legs tensed.

Tsuki

Punch forms are called "tsuki". (Zuki when used with punch name.) This lesson covers 7 basic tsukis:

1. Seiken Zuki
2. Tate Zuki
3. Ura Zuki
4. Ura Uchi
5. Age Zuki
6. Furi Zuki
7. Kagi Zuki
8. Morote Zuki
9. Nukite

How to make your fist (akken)

Close fingers and stick out thumbs.

Curl all fingers except thumbs inside palm. Ensure fingers are curled in all the way.

Bend thumbs in over fingers.

Lesson 4: Punches (Tsuki)

1. Seiken Zuki

With fist near the hip, face palm upwards, and twist the fist inward as you punch. The process of twisting the fist allows for more strength when punching. By punching without opening too much space on the sides, you are able to throw a straight punch. The elbow should scrape the body as the punch is being thrown.

The knuckles on the index and middle fingers are used during the punch. The knuckles are also called daikentou.

Good: From the beginning of your hand to the finger tips, the arms should be straight.

Bad: Fist is not straight.

Lesson 4: Punches (Tsuki)
2. Tate Zuki

As with seiken zuki, punch without opening too much space on the sides, but this time, don't twist the fist all the way. Stop the punch with palm and fist faced sideways. This punch can be used with a snap of the wrist or with a straight thrusting motion.

3. Ura Zuki

Punch by raising fist from bottom upwards. This is basically an upper cut, and there are two types.

It's called ura zuki when a low punch is thrown and the palm is facing upwards (middle photo).

It's also called age zuki (right photo) when the punch is high. (Age is pronounced "ahh-ghe".)

Lesson 4: Punches (Tsuki)
4. Ura Uchi

Using the same fist as seiken, throw knuckles outwards with fingers facing body. (Snap fist like a whip.)

5. Age Zuki

Punching by raising your fist. Punch/attack by defending the jodan (face portion). Or use this punch when attacking from opponents blind spot to jodan area.

Lesson 4: Punches (Tsuki)
6. Furi Zuki

Swing your hands from the side as if throwing a hook punch in boxing. Swing hips after target is hit. The circular motion of punch allows for a strong punch.

This motion gives room for no guard but it delivers a strong punch. The target is predominantly in the front.

Lesson 4: Punches (Tsuki)
7. Kagi Zuki

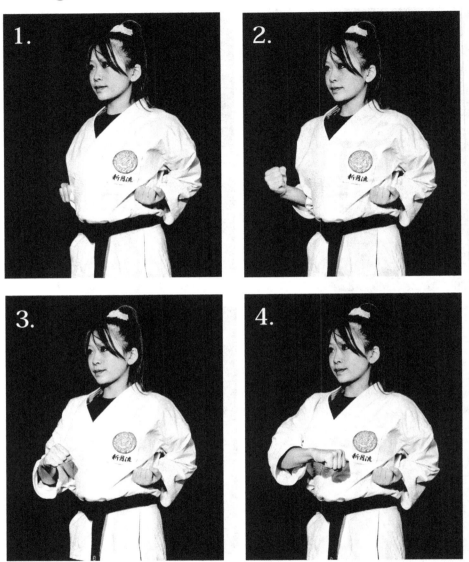

Very similar to furi zuki but instead of making a big circular motion, start with the elbow bent and fist placed relatively close to the body. The target in furi zuki is predominantly in front of you but in kagi zuki, the target is usually to your side.

Lesson 4: Punches (Tsuki)
8. Morote Zuki

The hand on the right should block the attack to the jodan while counter-attacking with age zuki. The lower hand should be positioned mid-level to go into ura zuki.

Attacking with both hands at the same time is called morote zuki. It is called suihei morote zuki when the attack is made mid-level.

9. Nukite

A punch using fingertips.

When a handshake is formed, it is called a tate nukite.

When the palm is faced down, it's called hira nukite.

Lesson 4: Punches (Tsuki)
Nukite in Action

Lesson 5: Kicks

Keri

Kicks are called "keri" or "geri" (when used to describe a specific kick). This lesson covers
two basic kicking forms:

1. Mae Geri
2. Mawashi Geri

Lesson 5: Kicks
1. Mae Geri

When standing on toes, the part that is left on the floor is the ball of the foot. Use the ball of the foot to kick forward. It is important to keep toes tightly pulled

1. Mae Geri (cont.)

back with the ankles straightened. Raise your legs adequately before kicking and quickly return to original stance after the kick is very important.

Lesson 5: Kicks (Keri)

5.

Lesson 5: Kicks (keri)
2. Mawashi Geri

The basic roundhouse kick entails raising the ankle and knee to the side and then kicking in a semi-circular motion. Kicking with the ball of the foot allows you to kick the target directly whereas kicking with the top of the foot gives you a wide range to kick your target. Try not to lean your body back too much.

Lesson 5: Kicks (keri)

How To Practice Kicking

**Bring your leg to the side and raise grab your ankle.
Let go of your hand and kick in a circular motion as if**

Lesson 5: Kicks (Keri)

you are drawing crescent moon. Bring back the kicking leg and grab the ankle.

 # Uke

Defensive blocks are callked "uke" (pronounced ooh-keh). This lesson will cover 8 basic block techniquies:

1. Soto Uke
2. Gedan Barai
3. Age Uke
4. Uchi Uke
5. Kakete Uke
6. Kentsui Uke
7. Shyutou Uke
8. Gedan Shyutou Uke

1. Soto Uke

Objective: To block attacks to the mid-section.

Movement: Block from inside to outside. From under the arm, make a fist where the palm is faced down and twist it as you move the shoulder forward.

Checkpoint: The distance between the elbow and the body should be a fist width. The fist should be the same height as the shoulder. Called 'hikite' , the other arm should be pulled back into proper position. When looking from the front, the elbow shouldn't be wider than where the ist is.

Hikite means to pull your hand back and place it to the side of your body. Engaging in hikite quickly allows for stronger, quicker attacks and blocks.

The palm of the fist should be faced up as you twist and ensure the pinky is touching the side of your body. It should be positioned above the belt (obi) with arm touching the sides of your body. Don't raise your shoulder.

Lesson 6: Blocks (uke)

1. Soto Uke

Lesson 6: Blocks (uke)

1. Soto Uke (Side View)

Lesson 6: Blocks (uke)

Lesson 6: Blocks (uke)
1. Soto Uke Kaishyu (open hands)

Kaishu means to open the hands, usually with the thumbs bent.

Lesson 6: Blocks (uke)

Soto Uke in Action: Block and Punch

Lesson 6: Blocks (uke)
2. Gedan Barai

Objective: To block attacks below the mid-section.

Movement: Place pinky from fist in front of shoulder.

Straighten your elbow as you make a sweeping motion.

The shoulder should be twisted forward at 45 degrees.

Lesson 6: Blocks (uke)

2. Gedan Barai (cont.)

Lesson 6: Blocks (uke)

Lesson 6: Blocks (uke)
Gedan Barai (side view)

Lesson 6: Blocks (uke)

Gedan Barai in Action: Block a Punch

Gedan Barai in Action: Block a Kick

Lesson 6: Blocks (uke)

3. Age Uke

Objective: To block attacks to the face.

Movement: Block with forearm and fist.

When your hand is in front of you, the inner part of arm will pass face.

When block is complete, pinky should be on top.

Block all the way above the head.

Lesson 6: Blocks (uke)

3. Age Uke (front view)

1.

2.

3.

4.

Lesson 6: Blocks (uke)

Lesson 6: Blocks (uke)

Lesson 6: Blocks (uke)
3. Age Uke (side view)

3. Age Uke (side view cont.)

Lesson 6: Blocks (uke)

Lesson 6: Blocks (uke)
Age Uke in Action

Lesson 6: Blocks (uke)
Bad Examples of Age Uke

The block is too low, allowing the opponent to attack head.

The face is not guarded, allowing an attack the face.

Lesson 6: Blocks (uke)

Too much tension in the hikite shoulder causing bad form.

Age uke should be an inside-out motion; not outside in like this.

Lesson 6: Blocks (uke)
4. Uchi Uke

Objective: To block attacks to the mid-section.

Movement: Block from outside to inside.

Block using forearm and fist.

The fist used to block will be brought from one side to the other side of the body, allowing for a complete block.

Lesson 6: Blocks (uke)

4. Uchi Uke (front view)

Lesson 6: Blocks (uke)

Lesson 6: Blocks (uke)

4. Uchi Uke (front view)

Lesson 6: Blocks (uke)

Twisting of the hand should be done like this.

The palm of the hand should be facing your face.

4. Uchi Uke (side view)

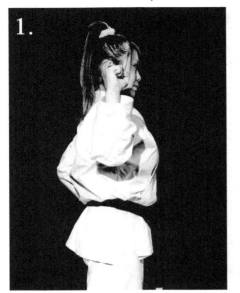

Lesson 6: Blocks (uke)

5.

6.

Lesson 6: Blocks (uke)
Uchi Uke in Action: Block a Punch

Lesson 6: Blocks (uke)

Lesson 6: Blocks (uke)

Lesson 6: Blocks (uke)

5. Kakete Uke (Also called kake uke)

Objective: Block attack to midsection and grab opponent's wrist.

Movement: With focus on the wrist, bring fingers outwards and block as you grab opponent's wrist and pull it close to you.

The other hand should be placed in front of your sides.

The palm should be faced down in kaishu mode.

Make sure the elbow isn't pointed outside (There should not be any space under your arm).

Lesson 6: Blocks (uke)

5. Kakete Uke (front view)

Lesson 6: Blocks (uke)

5.

6.

7.

8.

Kakete Uke in Action: Block to Kick

Lesson 6: Blocks (uke)

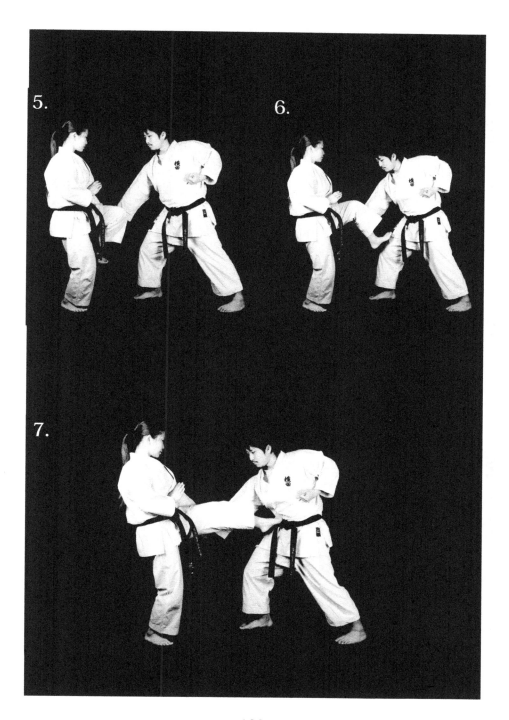

5.

6.

7.

Lesson 6: Blocks (uke)

6. Kentsui Uke (Also called tettsui)

Objective: To block a punch by hitting it downwards. Tsui uchi means "hammer hit".

Movement: Put hand out like a handshake and make a fist (called tatekentsui). Swing fist down onto opponent's arm, in a twisting motion. This causes opponent to lose balance.

This move is an effective way to break free from an opponent when grabbed by the sleeve.

6. Kentsui Uke

Lesson 6: Blocks (uke)

Lesson 6: Blocks (uke)
Kentsui Uke in Action: Block a Punch

Lesson 6: Blocks (uke)

Lesson 6: Blocks (uke)

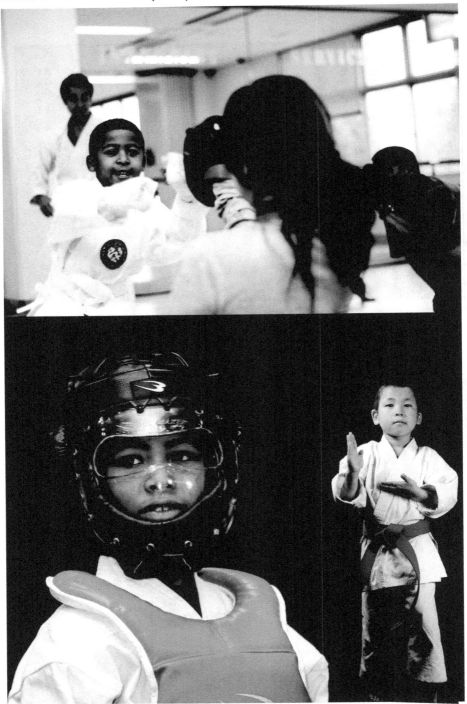

Lesson 6: Blocks (uke)

7. Shyutou Uke

Objective: Chop block

Movement: The portion from the base of the pinky finger to the wrist is called shyutou.

Place your pinky on your shoulder as you twist it to face outwards in front.

Chop with fingertips facing upwards.

Lesson 6: Blocks (uke)

7. Shyutou Uke (front view)

Lesson 6: Blocks (uke)

7. Shyutou Uke (front view cont.)

7. Shyutou Uke (side view)

Lesson 6: Blocks (uke)

7. Shyutou Uke (side view cont.)

Lesson 6: Blocks (uke)

Lesson 6: Blocks (uke)

Shyutou Uke in Action: Block a Punch

1.

2.

3.

Lesson 6: Blocks (uke)

Lesson 6: Blocks (uke)

Lesson 6: Blocks (uke)

8. Gedan Shyutou Uke

Obective: To block attack to groin. This move can be sued to grab an opponent's ankle or wrist and push him or her away.

Movement: The hand movement is the same as gedan barai. Turn with elbow and make sure there is no space between underarm.

Lesson 6: Blocks (uke)

8. Gedan Shyutou Uke

Lesson 6: Blocks (uke)

8. Gedan Shyutou Uke(cont.)

Lesson 6: Blocks (uke)

Shihou

Shihou is the very first kata or "form" that is taught at Shingetsuryu Karate School. Even beginners of karate should be able to enjoy this kata that I made. Before we get started, let me point out some quick tips.

Quick Points:
1. Stance is always Zenkutsu Dachi.
2. Two moves only (Chuudan Soto Uke and Chuudan Gyaku Zuki)
3. Do a block pose (soto uke) immediately after each attack.
4. Pivot foot will alternate by right, left, right, left.
5. While facing forward, movement direction will be left, right, front, back and front.
6. After each soto uke, there is a chuudan zuki and then a turn.

Lesson 7 Kata (Shihou)

◆ **Direction:** South
◆ **Name of skill:** Preparation
◆ **Stance :** Musubi Dachi
◆ **Point to see:** South
◆ **Right hand:** Open palm setit on your side.
◆ **Left hand:** Same as right
◆ **Right foot:** Open wide at 30-45 degree angle
◆ **Left foot:**S amea sr ight foot
◆ **Move:** Still
◆ **Purpose:** Prepare for kata
◆ **Remarks:** Relax shoulders

◆ **Direction:** South
◆ **Name of skill:** Rei
◆ **Stance:** Musubi Dachi
◆ **Point to see:** 3 meters below
◆ **Right hand:** Open palm and set it on your side
◆ **Left hand:** Same as right
◆ **Right foot:** As is
◆ **Left foot:** As is
◆ **Move:** Bow
◆ **Purpose:** Prepare for Kata
◆ **Remarks:** Don't say anything

◆ **Direction:** South
◆ **Name of skill:** Vocalizing name of Kata
◆ **Stance:** Musubi Dachi
◆ **Point to see:** South
◆ **Right hand:** On side of body
◆ **Left hand:** On side of body
◆ **Right foot:** Open wide at 30-45 degree angle
◆ **Left foot:** Same as right
◆ **Move:** Say "Shihou!"
◆ **Purpose:** Saying name of kata to perform
◆ **Remarks:** After bowing, take one deep breath then say the kata out loud

166

Lesson 7 Kata (Shihou)

◆ **Direction:** South
◆ **Point to see:** South
◆ **Right hand:** Cross both wrists
◆ **Left hand:** Same as right hand
◆ **Right foot:** As is
◆ **Left foot:** As is

◆ **Direction:** South
◆ **Name of skill:** Kamae (Pose)
◆ **Stance:** Hachiji Dachi
◆ **Point to see:** South
◆ **Right hand:** Make a fist
◆ **Left hand:** Same as right
◆ **Right foot:** Open wide at 30-45 degree angle
◆ **Left foot:** Same as right
◆ **Move:** Hold still for 2 seconds
◆ **Purpose:** Posing to prepare to fight
◆ **Remarks:** Leave one to two fist spaces in betweentwo hands

◆ **Direction:** South to East
◆ **Point to see:** South
◆ **Right hand:** Set on your right (put under right underarm)
◆ **Left hand:** From right underarm, move to front of left shoulder
◆ **Right foot:** As is
◆ **Left foot:** Take a big step to the East
◆ **Move:** Move swiftly

167

Lesson 7 Kata (Shihou)

- ◆ **Direction**: South to East
- ◆ **Point to see**: South
- ◆ **Right hand**: Set on your right (put under right underarm)
- ◆ **Left hand**: From right underarm, move to front of left shoulder
- ◆ **Right foot**: As is
- ◆ **Left foot**: Take a big step to the East
- ◆ **Move**: Move swiftly

- ◆ **Direction**: East
- ◆ **Name of skill**: Chuudan Soto Uke
- ◆ **Stance**: Left Zenkutsu Dachi
- ◆ **Point to see**: South
- ◆ **Right hand**: Set to the right of your body
- ◆ **Left hand**: In front of shoulder
- ◆ **Right foot**: Bend deep
- ◆ **Left foot**: Straighten leg out
- ◆ **Move**: Quick Pause
- ◆ **Purpose**: Receive chuudan zuki
- ◆ **Remarks**: Receive chuudan zuki

Lesson 7 Kata (Shihou)

◆ **Direction:** East
◆ **Point to see:** East
◆ **Right hand:** Attack as you're scraping your elbow against your body
◆ **Left hand:** Pull back your elbow as you scrape it against your body

◆ **Direction:** East
◆ **Name of skill:** Right Gyaku Zuki
◆ **Stance:** Left Zenkutsu Dachi
◆ **Point to see:** East
◆ **Right hand:** Chuudan Zuki
◆ **Left hand:** Hikite
◆ **Right foot:** Straighten leg out
◆ **Left foot:** Bend legs under shin perpendicularly
◆ **Move:** Twist your hips to the east and point your navel to the east
◆ **Purpose:** Attack to the mid section
◆ **Remarks:** Punch the mid section
◆ **Analysis:** Once attacked, counter-attack with gyaku zuki

Lesson 7 Kata (Shihou)

- ◆ **Direction:** Turn from east to west
- ◆ **Point to see:** East to West
- ◆ **Right hand:** Place snuggly under right elbow
- ◆ **Left hand:** Move it forward before securing it under the left underarm
- ◆ **Right foot:** Slide it to the North
- ◆ **Left foot:** Pivot
- ◆ **Move:** Move swiftly

- ◆ **Direction:** West
- ◆ **Name of skill:** Chuudan Soto Uke
- ◆ **Stance:** Right Zenkutsu Dachi
- ◆ **Point to see:** West
- ◆ **Right hand:** In front of shoulder
- ◆ **Left hand:** Place on left side of body
- ◆ **Right foot:** Bend deep
- ◆ **Left foot:** Quick Pause
- ◆ **Move:** Quick Pause
- ◆ **Purpose:** Receive chuudan zuki

Lesson 7 Kata (Shihou)

◆ **Direction:** West
◆ **Point to see:** West
◆ **Right hand:** Pull back as you scrape your elbow against your body
◆ **Left hand:** Attack as you scrape your elbow against your body

◆ **Direction:** West
◆ **Name of skill:** Left Gyaku Zuki
◆ **Stance:** Right Zenkutsu Dachi
◆ **Point to see:** West
◆ **Right hand:** Hikite
◆ **Left hand:** Chuudan Zuki
◆ **Right foot:** Bend Deep
◆ **Left foot:** Straighten leg out
◆ **Move:** Twist your hips to the west and point your navel to the west
◆ **Purpose:** Attack to the mid section
◆ **Remarks:** Punch the mid section

Lesson 7 Kata (Shihou)

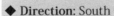

- ◆ **Direction:** Turn from West to South
- ◆ **Point to see:** West to South
- ◆ **Right hand:** Move it forward before securing it under the left underarm
- ◆ **Left hand:** Place snuggly under right underarm
- ◆ **Left foot:** Step in to the south
- ◆ **Move:** Move swiftly

- ◆ **Direction:** South
- ◆ **Name of skill:** Chuudan Soto Uke
- ◆ **Stance:** Right Zenkutsu dachi
- ◆ **Point to see:** South
- ◆ **Right hand:** In front of shoulder
- ◆ **Left hand:** Place on left side of body
- ◆ **Right foot:** Bend deep
- ◆ **Left foot:** Straighten leg out

172

Lesson 7 Kata (Shihou)

◆ **Direction**: South
◆ **Point to see:** South
◆ **Right hand:** Pull back as you scrape your elbow against your body
◆ **Left hand:** Attack as you scrape your elbow against your body

◆ **Direction:** South
◆ **Name of skill:** Right Gyaku Zuki
◆ **Stance:** Left Zenkutsu Dachi
◆ **Point to see:** South
◆ **Right hand:** Chuudan Zuki
◆ **Left hand:** Hikite
◆ **Right foot:** Straighten leg out
◆ **Left foot:** Bend Deep
◆ **Move:** The navel should face south
◆ **Purpose:** Attack to mid section
◆ **Remarks:** Punch the mid section

◆ **Direction:** Turn from South to North
◆ **Point to see:** South to North
◆ **Right hand:** Place snuggly under left elbow
◆ **Left hand:** Move it forward before securing it under the right underarm
◆ **Right foot:** Slide in to the East
◆ **Left foot:**
◆ **Move:** Move swiftly

Lesson 7 Kata (Shihou)

◆ **Direction:** North
◆ **Name of skill:** Chuudan Soto Uke
◆ **Stance:** Right Zenkutsu dachi
◆ **Point to see:** North
◆ **Right hand:** In front of shoulder
◆ **Left hand:** Place on left side of body
◆ **Right foot:** Bend deep
◆ **Left foot:** Straighten leg out

◆ **Direction:** North
◆ **Name of Skill:**
◆ **Stance :**
◆ **Point to See:** North
◆ **Right Hand :** Pull back as you scrape your elbow against your body
◆ **Left Hand:** Attack as you scrape your elbow against your body

Lesson 7 Kata (Shihou)

- ◆ **Direction:** North
- ◆ **Name of Skill:** Left Gyakuzuki
- ◆ **Stance:** Right Zenkutsu Dachi
- ◆ **Point to See:** North
- ◆ **Right Hand:** Hikite
- ◆ **Left Hand:** Chuudan Zuki
- ◆ **Right Foot:** Bend Deep
- ◆ **Left Foot:** Straighten leg out
- ◆ **Move:** Navel should face the north
- ◆ **Purpose:** Attack to mid section
- ◆ **Remarks:** Punch mid section

- ◆ **Direction:** Turn from north to south
- ◆ **Name of Skill:**
- ◆ **Stance:**
- ◆ **Point to See:** North to south
- ◆ **Right Hand:** Move it forward before securing it under left underarm
- ◆ **Left Hand:** Place snuggly under right elbow
- ◆ **Right Foot:** Pivot
- ◆ **Left Foot:** Slide to the East
- ◆ **Move:** Move swiftly

Lesson 7 Kata (Shihou)

◆ **Direction:** South
◆ **Name of Skill:** Chuudan Soto Uke
◆ **Stance:** Left Zenkutsu Dachi
◆ **Point to See:** South
◆ **Right Hand:** Place on right side of body
◆ **Left Hand:** In front of shoulder
◆ **Right Foot:** Straighten leg out
◆ **Left Foot:** Bend deep
◆ **Move:** Quick pause
◆ **Purpose:** Receive chuudan zuki

◆ **Direction:** South
◆ **Name of Skill**
◆ **Stance:**
◆ **Point to See:** South
◆ **Right Hand:** Attack as you scrape your elbow against your body
◆ **Left Hand:** Pulll back as you scrape your elbow against your body

Lesson 7 Kata (Shihou)

◆ **Direction:** South
◆ **Name of Skill:** Right gyaku zuki, Kiai
◆ **Stance:** Left zenkutsu dachi
◆ **Point to See:** South
◆ **Right Hand:** Chuudan zuki
◆ **Left Hand:** Hikite
◆ **Right Foot:** Straighten leg out
◆ **Left Foot:** Bend deep
◆ **Move:** Shout "Ei!" as you attack and pause for 2~3 seconds
◆ **Purpose:** Attack to mid section

◆ **Direction:** South
◆ **Stance:** From left zenkutsu dachi to hachiji dachi
◆ **Point to See:** South
◆ **Right Hand:** Cross with left wrist as you pull arm back
◆ **Left Hand:** Slightly move it forward as you cross it with right wrist
◆ **Right Foot:** As is
◆ **Left Foot:** Place right next to right foot then slide it to the east
◆ **Move:** Move slowly

◆ **Direction:** South
◆ **Name of Skill:** Pose
◆ **Stance:** Hachiji Dachi
◆ **Point to See:** South
◆ **Right Hand:** In front of body
◆ **Left Hand:** In front of body
◆ **Move:** Pause
◆ **Purpose:** End of kata
◆ **Remarks:** Imagining the end of a fight

Lesson 7 Kata (Shihou)

- ◆ **Direction:** South
- ◆ **Stance:** From hachiji dachi to musubi dachi
- ◆ **Point to See:** South
- ◆ **Right Hand:** Open palm as you move it to the side of body
- ◆ **Left Hand:** Same as right hand
- ◆ **Right Foot:** Place next to right foot and touch the heels together
- ◆ **Left Foot:** As is
- ◆ **Purpose:** Move slowly

- ◆ **Direction:** South
- ◆ **Name of Skill:** Rei
- ◆ **Stance:** Musubi dachi
- ◆ **Point to See:** Bowing from the south, look 3 meters down and stand straight up
- ◆ **Right Hand:** Place on side of body
- ◆ **Left Hand:** Same as right hand
- ◆ **Move:** Bow slowly
- ◆ **Purpose:** Signifies the end of the kata
- ◆ **Remarks:** The end of the kata

Shihou Main Steps

This section excludes the in-between strokes and explanation and rather explains it with just its main moves. For explanation of each move, please refer to the complete portion of shihou.

Once you grasp the meaning of the kata, you should be able to come to this portion of the kata for reference.

Lesson 7: Kata (Shihou)

Lesson 7: Kata (Shihou)

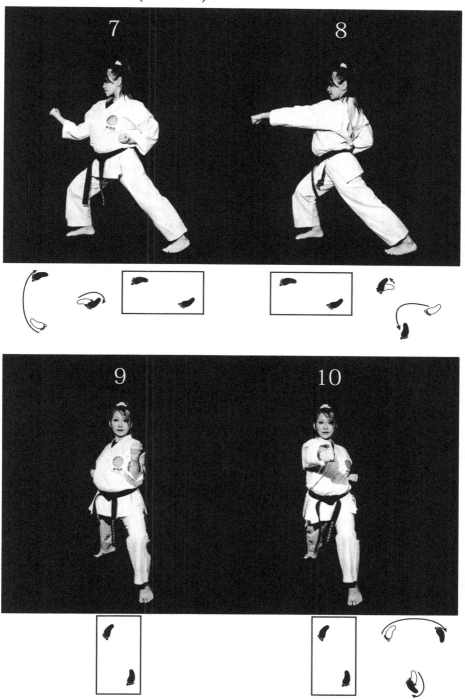

Lesson 7: Kata (Shihou)

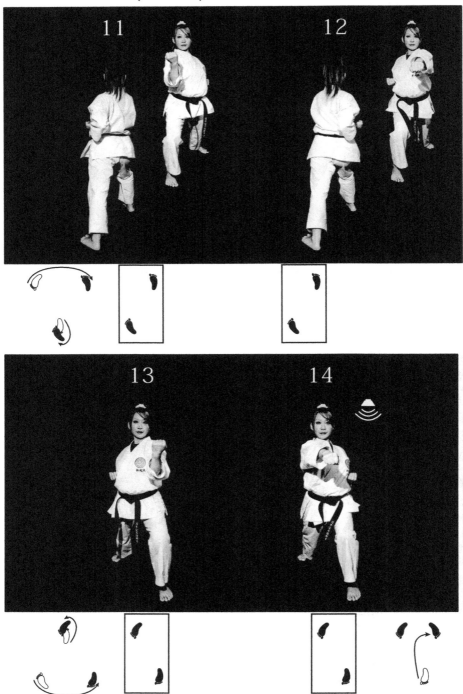

Lesson 7: Kata (Shihou)

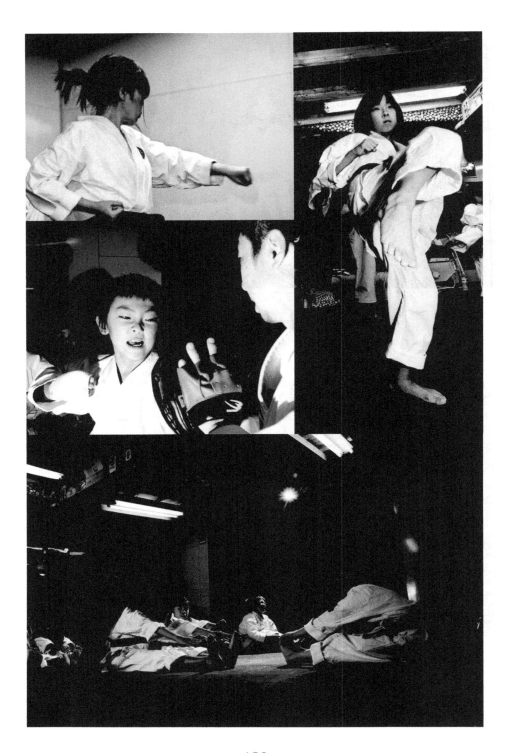

Lesson 8: Kata

# Heian Nidan

Heian (also can be read as Pinan) kata consists of shodan, nidan, sandan, yodan and godan. Kenwa Mabuni, the founder of Shitoryu Karate, declared reading it as "Heian".

The heian kata is said to have been created by Itosu Ankou sensei, from shodan to godan, all having its own unique technique. When a beginner learns all five of this kata, he/she incorporates the basic moves of all the karate forms into his/her body.

Heian shodan is more difficult than heian nidan, thus most dojos teach the heaian nidan first.

Heian nidan includes basic stances like neko ashi dachi, moto dachi, zenkutsu dachi, shiko dachi. Be careful not to lose balance when moving and keep in mind to keep the head still.

Lesson 8: Kata [Heian Nidan (Pinan Nidan)]

◆ **Direction:** South
◆ **Name of skill:** Preparation
◆ **Stance:** Musubi Dachi
◆ **Point to see:** South
◆ **Right hand:** Open palm and set it on your side.
◆ **Left hand:** Same as right
◆ **Right foot:** Open wide at a 30-45 degree angle
◆ **Left foot:** Same as right foot
◆ **Move:** Still
◆ **Purpose:** Prepare for kata
◆ **Remarks:** Relax shoulders

◆ **Direction:** South
◆ **Name of skill:** Rei
◆ **Stance:** Musubi Dachi
◆ **Point to see:** Diagonally
◆ **Right hand:** Open palm and set it on your side
◆ **Left hand:** Same as right
◆ **Right foot:** As is
◆ **Left foot:** As is
◆ **Move:** Bow
◆ **Purpose:** Prepare for kata
◆ **Remarks:** Don't say anything

◆ **Direction:** South
◆ **Name of skill:** Vocalizing name of Kata
◆ **Stance:** Musubi Dachi
◆ **Point to see:** South
◆ **Right hand:** On side of body
◆ **Left hand:** On side of body
◆ **Right foot:** Open wide at 30-45 degree angle
◆ **Left foot:** Same as right
◆ **Move:** Say "Heian Nidan!"
◆ **Purpose:** Saying name of Kata to perform
◆ **Remarks:** After bowing, take one deep breath and then say the kata out loud

Lesson 8: Kata [Heian Nidan (Pinan Nidan)]

- ◆ **Direction**: South
- ◆ **Point to See**: South
- ◆ **Right hand**: Cross both wrists
- ◆ **Left hand**: Same as right hand
- ◆ **Right foot**: Move west
- ◆ **Left foot**: As is
- ◆ **Move**: Move slowly

- ◆ **Direction**: South
- ◆ **Name of skill**: Pose
- ◆ **Stance**: Hachiji Dachi
- ◆ **Point to see**: South
- ◆ **Right hand**: Make a fist
- ◆ **Left hand**: Same as right
- ◆ **Right foot**: Open wide at 30-45 degree angle
- ◆ **Left foot**: Same as right
- ◆ **Move**: Hold still for 2 seconds
- ◆ **Purpose**: Posing to prepare to fight
- ◆ **Remarks**: Leave one to two fist spaces in between two hands

- ◆ **Direction**: From south to east
- ◆ **Stance**: From hachiji dachi to neko ashi dachi
- ◆ **Point to see**: East
- ◆ **Right hand**: Right side of body (place under right underarm)
- ◆ **Left hand**: Move in a circular motion as if hitting something with a hammer
- ◆ **Right foot**: As is, bend knee deep
- ◆ **Left foot**: Pull slightly back to the west and raise the heel
- ◆ **Move**: Move swiftly

Lesson 8: Kata [Heian Nidan (Pinan Nidan)]

◆ **Direction:** East
◆ **Name of skill:** Jyodan Kent-sui Uke
◆ **Stance:** Left Neko ashi dachi
◆ **Point to see:** East
◆ **Right hand:** On right side of body
◆ **Left hand:** Straighten arm and place in front of shoulder
◆ **Right foot:** Bend deep
◆ **Left foot:** Raise heel high
◆ **Move:** Quick pause
◆ **Purpose:** Receive upper punch

◆ **Direction:** East
◆ **Stance:** From left neko ashi dachi to right zenkutsu dachi
◆ **Point to see:** East
◆ **Right hand:** Punch
◆ **Left hand:** Hikite
◆ **Right foot:** Place next to left foot and step forward
◆ **Left foot:** As is
◆ **Move:** Move quickly
◆ **Remarks:** Keep upper body still as you move. Your body should be low when moving

Lesson 8: Kata [Heian Nidan (Pinan Nidan)]

- ◆ **Direction**: East
- ◆ **Name of skill**: Oi zuki
- ◆ **Stance**: Right zenkutsu dachi
- ◆ **Point to see**: East
- ◆ **Right hand**: Punch to the mid section
- ◆ **Left hand**: Pull under left underarm
- ◆ **Right foot**: Bend deep
- ◆ **Left foot**: Straighten leg out
- ◆ **Move**: Quick pause
- ◆ **Purpose**: Attack the mid section

- ◆ **Direction**: From east to west
- ◆ **Point to see**: From east to west
- ◆ **Right hand**: Pull back to top of shoulder
- ◆ **Left hand**: Place under right underarm
- ◆ **Right foot**: Place next to left foot
- ◆ **Left foot**: Rotate from ball of foot (pivot)
- ◆ **Move**: Rotate swiftly

Lesson 8: Kata [Heian Nidan (Pinan Nidan)]

◆ **Direction:** West
◆ **Name of skill:** Gedan barai
◆ **Stance:** Zenkutsu dachi
◆ **Point to see:** West
◆ **Right hand:** Gedan barai (Lower it by 45 degrees)
◆ **Left hand:** Hikite
◆ **Right foot:** Bend deep
◆ **Left foot:** Straighten leg out
◆ **Move:** Quick Pause
◆ **Purpose:** Guarding the lower half of body

◆ **Direction:** West
◆ **Stance:** From right zenkutsu dachi to right moto dachi
◆ **Point to see:** West
◆ **Right hand:** From gedan barai to kentsui uke
◆ **Left hand:** As is
◆ **Right foot:** Take a small step back and bend deep
◆ **Left foot:** Straighten leg out
◆ **Move:** Move swiftly

Lesson 8: Kata [Heian Nidan (Pinan Nidan)]

◆ **Direction:** West
◆ **Name of skill:** Kentsui uke
◆ **Stance:** Motodachi
◆ **Point to see:** West
◆ **Right hand:** Extend it to shoulder length high
◆ **Left hand:** Hikite
◆ **Right foot:** Bend deep
◆ **Left foot:** Straighten leg out
◆ **Move:** Quick pause
◆ **Purpose:** Receive jodan zuki by rotating arm

◆ **Direction:** West
◆ **Stance:** From right moto dachi to left zenkutsu dachi
◆ **Point to see:** West
◆ **Right hand:** Hikite
◆ **Left hand:** Chuudan zuki
◆ **Right foot:** As is
◆ **Left foot:** Place next to right foot and step forward
◆ **Move:** Move swiftly

Lesson 8: Kata [Heian Nidan (Pinan Nidan)]

◆ **Direction:** West
◆ **Stance:** From right moto dachi to left zenkutsu dachi
◆ **Point to see:** West
◆ **Right hand:** Hikite
◆ Left hand: Chuudan zuki
◆ **Right foot:** As is
◆ **Left foot:** Place next to right foot and step forward
◆ **Move:** Move swiftly

◆ **Direction:** West
◆ **Name of skill:** Chuudan Zuki
◆ **Stance:** Zenkutsu Dachi
◆ **Point to see:** West
◆ **Right hand:** Hikite
◆ **Left hand:** Punch mid section
◆ **Right foot:** Straighten leg out
◆ **Left foot:** Bend deep
◆ **Move:** Quick pause
◆ **Purpose:** Attack mid section

Lesson 8: Kata [Heian Nidan (Pinan Nidan)]

- ◆ **Direction:** From west to south
- ◆ **Stance:** From left zenkutsu dachi to left zenkutsu dachi
- ◆ **Point to see:** From west to south
- ◆ **Right hand:** Hikite
- ◆ **Left hand:** Gedan barai
- ◆ **Right foot:** Straighten leg out
- ◆ **Left foot:** Bend deep
- ◆ **Move:** Move swiftly

Lesson 8: Kata [Heian Nidan (Pinan Nidan)]

◆ **Direction**: South
◆ **Stance**: From left zenkutsu dachi to left zenkutsu dachi
◆ **Point to see**: From west to south
◆ **Right hand**: Hikite
◆ **Left hand**: Gedan barai
◆ **Right foot**: Straighten leg out
◆ **Left foot**: Bend deep
◆ **Move**: Quick pause
◆ **Purpose**: Sweep opponent's kick and block

Lesson 8: Kata [Heian Nidan (Pinan Nidan)]

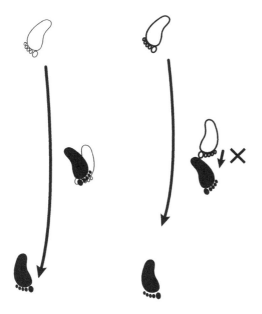

◆ **Direction:** South
◆ **Stance:** Repetitive zen-kutsu dachi
◆ **Point to see:** South
◆ **Right hand:** Raise it
◆ **Left hand:** Hikite
◆ **Right foot:** Place next to left foot and step forward
◆ **Left foot:** Move as knee is bent deep
◆ **Move:** Move swiftly while body is positioned low
◆ **Remarks:** Don't slide the pivot foot

Lesson 8: Kata [Heian Nidan (Pinan Nidan)]

◆ **Direction**: South
◆ **Name of skill**: Right age uke
◆ **Stance**: Zenkutsu dachi
◆ **Point to see**: South
◆ **Right hand**: Block the jodan (face)
◆ **Left hand**: Hikite
◆ **Right foot**: Bend deep
◆ **Left foot**: Straighten leg out
◆ **Move**: Quick pause
◆ **Purpose**: Block attacks to the face
◆ **Remarks**: Don't hyper extend the right elbow. Cover as much of your face as possible

◆ **Direction**: South
◆ **Stance**: From zenkutsu dachi to zenkutsu dachi
◆ **Point to see**: South
◆ **Left hand**: Age uke
◆ **Right foot**: Move as knee is bent deep
◆ **Left foot**: Place next to right foot and step forward
◆ **Move**: Move swiftly while body is low
◆ **Remarks**: Leave right hand in blocking position ensuring face is covered

Lesson 8: Kata [Heian Nidan (Pinan Nidan)]

◆ **Direction:** South
◆ **Name of skill:** Age uke
◆ **Stance:** Zenkutsu dachi
◆ **Point to see:** South
◆ **Right hand:** Hikite
◆ **Left hand:** Age uke
◆ **Right foot:** Straighten leg out
◆ **Left foot:** Bend deep
◆ **Move:** Quick pause then immediately go to next step
◆ **Purpose:** Block attack to the face

◆ **Direction:** South
◆ **Name of skill:** Repetitive age uke
◆ **Stance:** From zenkutsu dachi to zenkutsu dachi
◆ **Point to see:** South
◆ **Right hand:** Age uke
◆ **Left hand:** Hikite
◆ **Right foot:** Place next to left foot and step forward
◆ **Left foot:** Move as knee is bent deep
◆ **Move:** Move swiftly while body is low
◆ **Remarks:** Leave left hand in blocking position ensuring face is covered

Lesson 8: Kata [Heian Nidan (Pinan Nidan)]

◆ **Direction:** South
◆ **Name of skill:** Age uke
◆ **Stance:** Zenkutsu dachi
◆ **Point to see:** South
◆ **Right hand:** Block the face
◆ **Left hand:** Hikite
◆ **Right foot:** Bend deep
◆ **Left foot:** Straighten leg out
◆ **Move:** Quick pause
◆ **Purpose:** Block attack to face

Lesson 8: Kata [Heian Nidan (Pinan Nidan)]

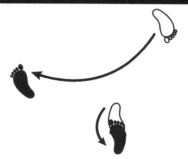

- ◆ **Direction:** From south to northwest
- ◆ **Stance:** From zenkutsu dachi to zenkutsu dachi
- ◆ **Point to see:** From south to northwest
- ◆ **Right hand:** Hikite
- ◆ **Left hand:** Raise to right shoulder and then sweep
- ◆ **Right foot:** Pivot foot
- ◆ **Left foot:** Swiftly slide to northwest
- ◆ **Move:** Swiftly rotate
- ◆ **Remarks:** Place left foot next to right foot first

Lesson 8: Kata [Heian Nidan (Pinan Nidan)]

◆ **Direction:** Northwest
◆ **Name of skill:** Gedan barai
◆ **Stance:** Zenkutsu dachi
◆ **Point to see:** Northwest
◆ **Right hand:** Hikite
◆ **Left hand:** Lower by 45 degrees, in front of thigh
◆ **Right foot:** Straighten leg out
◆ **Left foot:** Bend deep towards northwest
◆ **Move:** Quick pause but immediately move to next step
◆ **Purpose:** Sweep block opponent's kick

◆ **Direction:** Northwest
◆ **Stance:** From zenkutsu dachi to zenkutsu dachi
◆ **Point to see:** Northwest
◆ **Right hand:** Punch
◆ **Left hand:** Hikite
◆ **Right foot:** Place next to left foot and step forward
◆ **Left foot:** As is
◆ **Move:** Move swiftly
◆ **Purpose:** Move as you're blocking with left hand

Lesson 8: Kata [Heian Nidan (Pinan Nidan)]

◆ **Direction:** Northwest
◆ **Name of skill:** Right (mid) oi zuki
◆ **Stance:** Right zenkutsu dachi
◆ **Point to see:** Northwest
◆ **Right hand:** Chuudan zuki
◆ **Left hand:** Hikite
◆ **Right foot:** Bend deep
◆ **Left foot:** Straighten leg out
◆ **Move:** Target opponent's vitals

Lesson 8: Kata [Heian Nidan (Pinan Nidan)]

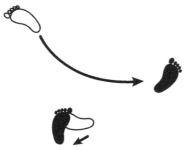

- ◆ **Direction:** From northwest to northeast
- ◆ **Stance:** From zenkutsu dachi to zenkutsu dachi
- ◆ **Point to see:** From northwest to northeast
- ◆ **Right hand:** Pull back to top of left shoulder
- ◆ **Left hand:** Pull under right underarm
- ◆ **Right foot:** Place next to left foot then step out to northeast
- ◆ **Left foot:** Twist from ball of foot
- ◆ **Move:** Move swiftly

Lesson 8: Kata [Heian Nidan (Pinan Nidan)]

- ◆ Direction: Northeast
- ◆ Name of skill: Gedan barai
- ◆ Stance: Zenkutsu dachi
- ◆ Point to see: Northeast
- ◆ Right hand: Gedan barai
- ◆ Left hand: Hikite
- ◆ Right foot: Bend deep
- ◆ Left foot: Straighten leg out
- ◆ Move: Quick pause but immediately go to next step
- ◆ Purpose: Sweep opponent's kick or attack to groin

- ◆ Direction: Northeast
- ◆ Stance: From right zenkutsu dachi to left zenkutsu dachi
- ◆ Point to see: Northeast
- ◆ Right hand: Hikite
- ◆ Left hand: Punch
- ◆ Right foot: As is
- ◆ Left foot: Place next to right foot and move forward
- ◆ Move: Move swiftly
- ◆ Remarks: Move as you block with right hand

Lesson 8: Kata [Heian Nidan (Pinan Nidan)]

- ◆ **Direction:** Northeast
- ◆ **Stance:** From right zenkutsu dachi to left zenkutsu dachi
- ◆ **Point to see:** Northeast
- ◆ **Right hand:** Hikite
- ◆ **Left hand:** Punch
- ◆ **Right foot:** As is
- ◆ **Left foot:** Place next to right foot and move forward
- ◆ **Move:** Move swiftly
- ◆ **Remarks:** Move as you block with right hand

Lesson 8: Kata [Heian Nidan (Pinan Nidan)]

◆ **Direction:** Northeast
◆ **Name of skill:** Chuudan oi zuki
◆ **Stance:** Zenkutsu dachi
◆ **Point to see:** Northeast
◆ **Right hand:** Hikite
◆ **Left hand:** Chuudan zuki
◆ **Right foot:** Straighten leg out
◆ **Left foot:** Bend deep
◆ **Move:** Quick pause
◆ **Purpose:** Attack opponent's vitals

◆ **Direction:** From northeast to north
◆ **Stance:** From left zenkutsu dachi to left zenkutsu dachi
◆ **Point to see:** Place under left underarm and lock it in place
◆ **Right hand:** Place on right shoulder then do a gedan barai
◆ **Left hand:** Pivot foot
◆ **Right foot:** Slide swiftly
◆ **Left foot:** Swiftly slide to the west
◆ **Move:** Move swiftly

Lesson 8: Kata [Heian Nidan (Pinan Nidan)]

◆ **Direction:** From northeast to north
◆ **Stance:** From left zenkutsu dachi to left zenkutsu dachi
◆ **Point to see:** Place under left underarm and lock it in place
◆ **Right hand:** Place on right shoulder then do a gedan barai
◆ **Left hand:** Pivot foot
◆ **Right foot:** Slide swiftly
◆ **Left foot:** Swiftly slide to the west
◆ **Move:** Move swiftly

Lesson 8: Kata [Heian Nidan (Pinan Nidan)]

◆ **Direction:** North
◆ **Name of skill:** Gedan barai
◆ **Stance:** Left zenkutsu dachi
◆ **Point to see:** North
◆ **Right hand:** Hikite
◆ **Left hand:** Lower by 45 degree
◆ **Right foot:** Straighten leg out
◆ **Left foot:** Bend deep
◆ **Move:** Quick pause
◆ **Purpose:** Sweep opponent's kick or attack to groin

◆ **Direction:** North
◆ **Stance:** From zenkutsu dachi to zenkutsu dachi
◆ **Point to see:** North
◆ **Right hand:** Punch
◆ **Left hand:** Hikite
◆ **Right foot:** Place next to left foot and then move forward
◆ **Left foot:** As is
◆ **Move:** Move swiftly as your body is positioned low

Lesson 8: Kata [Heian Nidan (Pinan Nidan)]

◆ **Direction:** North
◆ **Stance:** From zenkutsu dachi to zenkutsu dachi
◆ **Point to see:** North
◆ **Right hand:** Punch
◆ **Left hand:** Hikite
◆ **Right foot:** Place next to left foot and then move forward
◆ **Left foot:** As is
◆ **Move:** Move swiftly as your body is positioned low

◆ **Direction:** North
◆ **Name of skill:** Right chuudan oi zuki
◆ **Stance:** Right zenkutsu dachi
◆ **Point to see:** North
◆ **Right hand:** Punch
◆ **Left hand:** Hikite
◆ **Right foot:** Bend deep
◆ **Left foot:** Straighten leg out
◆ **Move:** Quick pause
◆ **Purpose:** Attack opponent's weak point

Lesson 8: Kata [Heian Nidan (Pinan Nidan)]

◆ **Direction:** North
◆ **Stance:** From zenkutsu dachi to zenkutsu dachi
◆ **Point to see:** North
◆ **Right hand:** Hikite
◆ **Left hand:** Punch
◆ **Right foot:** As is
◆ **Left foot:** Place next to right foot and move forward
◆ **Move:** Move swiftly as body is positioned low
◆ **Purpose:** Leave right punch movement as is and move

Lesson 8: Kata [Heian Nidan (Pinan Nidan)]

◆ **Direction:** North
◆ **Name of skill:** Left chuudan oi zuki
◆ **Stance:** Left zenkutsu dachi
◆ **Point to see:** North
◆ **Right hand:** Hikite
◆ **Left hand:** Punch
◆ **Right foot:** Straighten leg out
◆ **Left foot:** Bend deep
◆ **Move:** Quick pause but immediately go to next step
◆ **Purpose:** Attack opponent's weak point

Lesson 8: Kata [Heian Nidan (Pinan Nidan)]

- ◆ **Direction:** North
- ◆ **Stance:** Zenkutsu dachi to zen-kutsu dachi
- ◆ **Point to see:** North
- ◆ **Right hand:** Punch
- ◆ **Left hand:** Hikite
- ◆ **Right foot:** Place next to left foot and move forward
- ◆ **Left foot:** As is
- ◆ **Move:** Move swiftly as body is positioned low
- ◆ **Remarks:** Leave left punch movement as is and move

- ◆ **Direction:** North
- ◆ **Name of skill:** Right chuudan oi zuki
- ◆ **Stance:** Right zenkutsu dachi
- ◆ **Point to see:** North
- ◆ **Right hand:** Punch
- ◆ **Left hand:** Hikite
- ◆ **Right foot:** Bend deep
- ◆ **Left foot:** Straighten leg out
- ◆ **Move:** Quick pause
- ◆ **Purpose:** Attack opponent's weak point
- ◆ **Remarks:** Shout "Ei!" with kiai as you attack

Lesson 8: Kata [Heian Nidan (Pinan Nidan)]

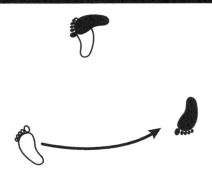

- ◆ **Direction:** From north to southeast
- ◆ **Stance:** From zenkutsu dachi to shiko dachi
- ◆ **Point to see:** From north to southeast
- ◆ **Right hand:** Cover your sides (weakpoint)
- ◆ **Left hand:** Pull back to front of right shoulder and then block with shuto
- ◆ **Right foot:** pivot foot
- ◆ **Left foot:** To southeast
- ◆ **Move:** Rotate swiftly

Lesson 8: Kata [Heian Nidan (Pinan Nidan)]

◆ **Direction:** Southeast
◆ **Name of skill:** Gedan shuto uke
◆ **Stance:** Shiko dachi
◆ **Point to see:** Southeast
◆ **Right hand:** Cover your sides (weakpoint)
◆ **Left hand:** Block with shuto
◆ **Right foot:** Bend deep
◆ **Left foot:** Bend deep
◆ **Move:** Quick pause then immediately go to next step

Lesson 8: Kata [Heian Nidan (Pinan Nidan)]

◆ **Direction**: Southeast
◆ **Stance**: Shiko dachi to shiko dachi
◆ **Point to see**: Southeast
◆ **Right hand**: Place in front of left shoulder and then chop
◆ **Left hand**: As is up until the right hand does the chop
◆ **Right foot**: To southeast
◆ **Left foot**: Pivot foot
◆ **Move**: Move forward swiftly
◆ **Remarks**: Move while your body is positioned low

Lesson 8: Kata [Heian Nidan (Pinan Nidan)]

- ◆ **Direction:** Southeast
- ◆ **Name of skill:** Gedan shuto uke
- ◆ **Stance:** Shiko dachi
- ◆ **Point to see:** Southeast
- ◆ **Right hand:** Shuto uke
- ◆ **Left hand:** Cover your sides (weak-point)
- ◆ **Right foot:** Bend deep
- ◆ **Left foot:** Bend deep
- ◆ **Move:** Quick pause
- ◆ **Purpose:** Block opponent's kick

- ◆ **Direction:** From southeast to southwest
- ◆ **Stance:** From shiko dachi to shiko dachi
- ◆ **Point to see:** Southwest
- ◆ **Right hand:** Shuto uke
- ◆ **Left hand:** Cover your sides (weak-point)
- ◆ **Right foot:** Swiftly slide to Southwest
- ◆ **Left foot:** Pivot foot
- ◆ **Move:** Move while your body is positioned low

Lesson 8: Kata [Heian Nidan (Pinan Nidan)]

◆ **Direction:** Southwest
◆ **Name of skill:** Gedan shuto uke
◆ **Stance:** Shiko dachi
◆ **Point to see:** Southwest
◆ **Right hand:** Shuto uke
◆ **Left hand:** Cover your sides (weak-point)
◆ **Right foot:** Bend deep
◆ **Left foot:** Bend deep
◆ **Move:** Quick pause but immediately go to next step
◆ **Purpose:** Block opponent's kick

Lesson 8: Kata [Heian Nidan (Pinan Nidan)]

◆ **Direction:** Southwest
◆ **Stance:** Shiko dachi to shiko dachi
◆ **Point to see:** Southwest
◆ **Right hand:** Place in front of left shoulder and then chop
◆ **Left hand:** As is up until the right hand does the chop
◆ **Right foot:** Pivot foot
◆ **Left foot:** To southwest
◆ **Move:** Move forward swiftly
◆ **Remarks:** Move while body is positioned low

◆ **Direction:** Southwest
◆ **Name of skill:** Gedan shuto uke
◆ **Stance:** Shiko dachi
◆ **Point to see:** Southwest
◆ **Right hand:** Cover your sides (weak point)
◆ **Left hand:** Shuto uke
◆ **Right foot:** Bend deep
◆ **Left foot:** Bend deep
◆ **Move:** Quick pause but immediately move to next step
◆ **Purpose:** Block opponent's kick

Lesson 8: Kata [Heian Nidan (Pinan Nidan)]

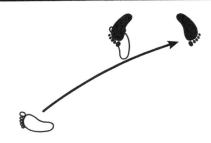

◆**Direction:** Southwest to south
◆**Name of Skill:** From gedan shuto uke to hachiji dachi
◆**Stance:** Hachiji dachi
◆**Point to see:** Southwest
◆**Right Hand:** Cross over left wrist
◆**Left Hand:** Cross with right wrist
◆**Right foot:** As is
◆**Left foot:** Step back and complete hachiji dachi
◆**Move:** Slowly move back into place
◆**Purpose:** End of fight

Lesson 8: Kata [Heian Nidan (Pinan Nidan)]

◆ **Direction:** South
◆ **Name of Skill:** Zanshin
◆ **Stance:** Hachiji dachi
◆ **Point to See:** Southwest
◆ **Right hand:** Place in front of you
◆ **Left hand:** Same as right hand
◆ **Right foot:** As is
◆ **Left foot:** As is
◆ **Move:** Move just the face southwest
◆ **Purpose:** After acknowledging the fight is over, look south

◆ **Direction:** South
◆ **Name of Skill:**
◆ **Stance:** From hachiji dachi to musubi dachi
◆ **Point to See:** South
◆ **Right hand:** Open palm and lower the arm
◆ **Left hand:** Same as right hand
◆ **Right foot:** Place next to left foot
◆ **Left foot:** As is

Lesson 8: Kata [Heian Nidan (Pinan Nidan)]

- ◆ **Direction**: South
- ◆ **Name of Skill**: Rei
- ◆ **Stance**: Musubi dachi
- ◆ **Point to See**: South
- ◆ **Right hand**: Place open hand on side of body
- ◆ **Left hand**: Same as right hand
- ◆ **Move**: Slowly lower head and hold in place for a second before raising it back up
- ◆ **Purpose**: End of kata
- ◆ **Remarks**: The end of kata

Heian Nidan (Pinan Nidan) Main Steps

This section excludes the in-between strokes and explanation and rather explains it with just its main moves. For explanation of each move, pleaserefer to the complete portion of heian nidan.

Once you grasp the meaning of the kata, you should be able to come to this portion of the kata for reference.

Lesson 8: Kata [Heian Nidan (Pinan Nidan)]

Lesson 8: Kata [Heian Nidan (Pinan Nidan)]

Lesson 8: Kata [Heian Nidan (Pinan Nidan)]

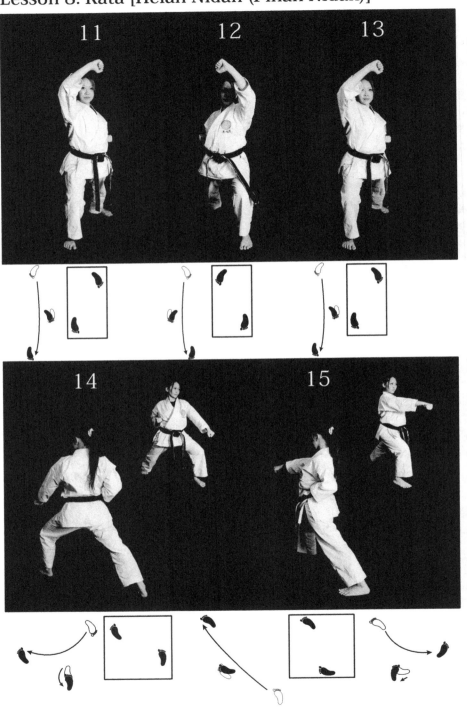

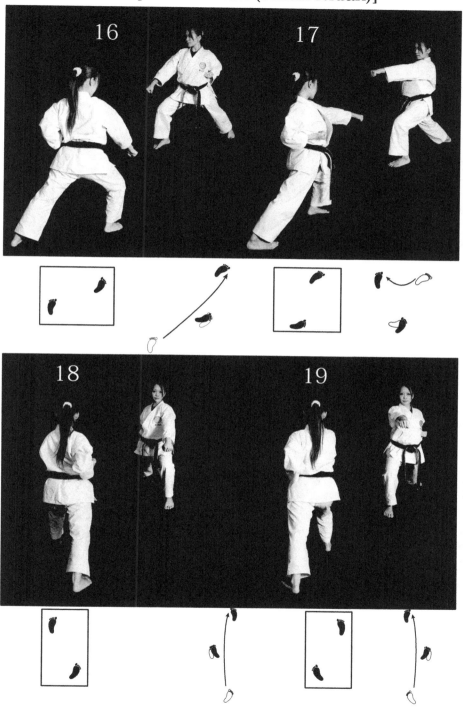

Lesson 8: Kata [Heian Nidan (Pinan Nidan)]

TRADITIONAL JAPANESE KARATE

ILLUSTRATING 227 TECHNIQUES
WITH EASY TERMINOLOGY

SHINGETSU-RYU KARATE
YASUSHI ABE

http://karatekid.info/

Made in the USA
Middletown, DE
24 July 2023

35673559R00136